P♥RN●FOR THE Bride

PORN FOR THE Bride

from the **CAMBRIDGE WOMEN'S PORNOGRAPHY COOPERATIVE**

photographs by **GRETCHEN LeMAISTRE**

CHRONICLE BOOKS

SAN FRANCISCO

A **PORN FOR** product.

PORN FOR™ is a trademark of Urgent Haircut Productions.

Library of Congress Cataloging-in-Publication Data available.
ISBN 978-0-8118-6927-0

Manufactured in China

Designed by Tracy Sunrize Johnson

MODELS: Eric O'Brien, David Mori, Eric Strom, Remington Hoffman,
Josh Stevenson, Edwin Black
MODELING AGENCIES: Boom, CityModel
ASSISTANTS: Kirk Crippens, Matt Szymankowski
STYLIST: Michah Bishop
ASSISTANT STYLIST: Ebony Haight
THE PHOTOGRAPHER WOULD LIKE TO THANK: Rosie and Yannic Friedman

10 9 8 7 6 5 4 3 2 1

Chronicle Books LLC
680 Second Street
San Francisco, California 94107

WWW.CHRONICLEBOOKS.COM

The perfect wedding. We all dream about it.

BUT WHAT ABOUT ACTUALLY PLANNING THE WEDDING?

The guest list, the seating chart, the expenses, the in-laws, the etiquette,
the thousands of important decisions left at your feet because

you're the only one who cares enough to make everything

PERFECT?

GIRLS, GIRLS, GIRLS! Raise your standards, please!
With the very book you hold in your hands, you can have the
GROOM OF YOUR DREAMS to help you. Want someone
who cares as much about the *flowers and vows* as he does about
the type of scotch at the open bar? He's right here in these pages.
Want a future husband who's man enough to assume the duties of the office
even before Day One? Look no further. Want a groom who insists on a
wholesome kayaking trip instead of strippers
for his bachelor party? Turn to page 18.

Haven't started your planning yet? **PERFECT.** Use this book to set the groom-ly standards. Already on your way? **GREAT.** Offer these scenarios as "helpful suggestions" to your soon-to-be spouse.

Been married for awhile? *No problem.*

SIMPLY REPLACE YOUR EXISTING, LAME MEMORIES WITH THESE CLASSIC SNAPSHOTS!

We at the **CAMBRIDGE WOMEN'S PORNOGRAPHY COOPERATIVE** have had girls in white dresses traipsing in and out of our labs for the better part of a year now. We listened carefully to their fantasies.

We concocted steamy scenarios to test our theories.

We honed and retested our conclusions. And we've compiled the explicit photographic evidence in this single volume.

We can say with 100% SCIENTIFIC CERTAINTY that these scenarios catch the bouquet. So sit back, put the *Martha Weddings* aside, pour yourself a glass of bubbly, and walk down the *Porn for the Bride* aisle . . . as many times as you like.

—*THE CAMBRIDGE WOMEN'S PORNOGRAPHY COOPERATIVE*

My Blue Heaven

Few people know of it; fewer still
In this rapidly shrinking world, there
even obscure; set apart in space and time; offe
Lakshadweep—the name comes out in a
although in fact there are just twenty-seven, ten of
Coast of India, this archipelago of atolls, coral reefs, and island
even Indian ones, don't note it. Yet for a dedicated group of members of

FRANCE

WHAT DO YOU THINK?

Castle in Ireland,

OR A PRIVATE ISLAND IN THE CARIBBEAN?

TELL ME HOW

You

IMAGINE

THE CEREMONY.

I DON'T THINK **$25,000** TO HAVE

Annie Leibovitz

PHOTOGRAPH THE WEDDING
IS TOO MUCH.

I BELIEVE IN TRADITION,
SO I'M ASKING YOUR FATHER
FOR YOUR HAND IN MARRIAGE.

Of course, if he says NO,
to hell with tradition!

Baby,

I **CAN'T WAIT** TO LOOK AT

china patterns

THIS WEEKEND.

IS IT OK IF I INVITE

your father and little brother

TO THE BACHELOR PARTY?
IT'S JUST A KAYAK TRIP WITH OLD FRIENDS,
AND A CHANCE TO TALK ABOUT

how lucky we all are.

IT'S THE GUEST BOOK.

I made it myself.

ADD **ANYONE YOU WANT**
TO THE GUEST LIST, BABE.

You're the only one

I'M GOING TO NOTICE
THAT DAY, ANYWAY.

Is there anything else
I can do around here,
so you can just *totally relax* and
focus on our big day?

Don't be silly.

You **don't need to exercise** before the wedding.

In fact, I think we need to put some wedding cake on you!

WELL, ROSES ARE CLASSIC . . .

but I really love the smell of the freesia.

WHAT DO **YOU** THINK?

YOU COULD WEAR

a burlap sack,

AND YOU'D STILL BE

more beautiful

THAN ANYONE ELSE AT THE WEDDING.

I feel it will be much more meaningful if we write our own vows.

I asked my buddy Paulie

to send me his toast in advance

so we could edit it.

You know how I worry

about my frat brothers

stepping over the line.

Of course

I can make sure there's a

GLUTEN-FREE MEAL

for your

great-uncle Melvin!

37

This is definitely an occasion for

NEW SHOES.

Since we only have

SIX MONTHS TO GO,

I invited the caterer

to cook for us all week.

Then we can

PICK OUR FAVORITES

for the wedding.

IT'S MY DAD.

HE THINKS THE

"bride's family pays"

IS A DUMB TRADITION,

AND HE WANTS TO

PICK UP THE WHOLE TAB.

SURE,

*invite **all** of your old boyfriends.*

LET 'EM GET ONE LAST LOOK AT

*what they're **missing!***

I DEVELOPED

A LITTLE

flowchart,

SO I

WON'T FORGET

ANY DETAILS.

I can't decide between the

GILL SANS LIGHT

or the

ARIAL NARROW

fonts.

I don't know if we

· · · · · · · · · · · · · · ·

TASTED ENOUGH **CAKES** THIS WEEKEND.

· · · · · · · · · · · · · · · · · · ·

Maybe we should start all over again?

I THINK IT'S HIGH TIME

I GOT RID OF **EVERY REMNANT** OF

my ex-girlfriends.

HON, I HAVE A LITTLE SURPRISE.

I'm heir to a pretty large fortune.

I WAITED TO TELL YOU UNTIL NOW,
BECAUSE I WANTED TO BE SURE

you loved me for me.

I TOOK A FIRST PASS
AT THE SEATING CHART.
I HOPE IT'S OK
THAT I DID A LITTLE

matchmaking

WITH OUR SINGLE FRIENDS.

Of course

I'M WEARING A RING.
I WANT EVERYONE TO KNOW

I'm taken!

I got you an

open account here at the spa.

If you feel the

SLIGHTEST BIT OF STRESS

between now and the wedding,

just go get yourself a

massage & a pedicure,

OK?

I THOUGHT
I'D GET A HEAD START
ADDRESSING THE

THANK-YOU

ENVELOPES.

We can write the notes
on the plane
and mail them
from our honeymoon.

I've got

FOUR OF MY COLLEGE FRIENDS

assigned to

YOUR MOTHER.

Their job is to make sure she

ALWAYS HAS A DANCE PARTNER.

Now,
just remember,

IF YOU START TO GET
OVERWHELMED
DURING THE CEREMONY,

just take my hands

AND

look into my eyes.

I picked up

the new

Martha

for you!

I'VE COME UP WITH A LIST OF TASKS
FOR BOTH OF OUR MOMS TO DO.

THIS SHOULD KEEP THEM

out of our hair

ON THE IMPORTANT STUFF
BETWEEN NOW AND THE WEDDING.

I GOT

you

AND

your best friend

TICKETS TO PARIS

SO YOU CAN PICK OUT A DRESS.

DON'T COME BACK WITHOUT

one you love!

I signed us up for

dance lessons.

I want my friends'
mouths to drop open
when they see me

twirl you.

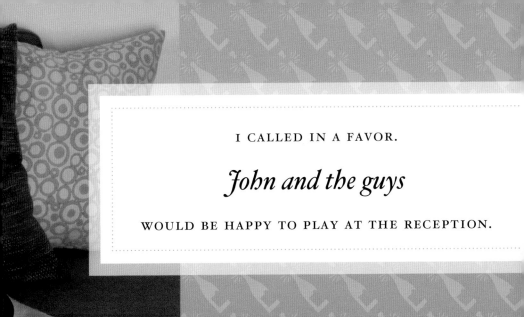

I CALLED IN A FAVOR.

John and the guys

WOULD BE HAPPY TO PLAY AT THE RECEPTION.

YOU'VE ALREADY GOT

TOO MUCH TO DO.

I'M HIRING A

personal shopper

TO FIND

the perfect shoes for your dress.

I've got it all loaded up
with the numbers of

EVERYONE EVEN REMOTELY
CONNECTED TO THE WEDDING.

If you need to reach

ANYONE

about

ANYTHING . . .

I've got you covered.

I'VE DECIDED

NOT TO INVITE

my cousin Andy.

I DON'T WANT TO

TAKE A CHANCE ON

ANYTHING

RUINING OUR BIG DAY.

No. I don't think

$5,000

is too much for a cake.

Are you getting enough

PREMARITAL PORN?

· ▷◁▷◁ ·

YOU SEE A NOTE HE'S WRITTEN TO HIMSELF TITLED "HONEYMOON CHECKLIST."
WHAT'S ON IT?

A. Chocolates, wine, fresh fruit, flowers. Every day.
B. Sight-seeing guidebook, SPF 75, nose hair trimmer, BlackBerry
C. Your sister's name, followed by a question mark

YOU'RE SHOWING HIM YOUR LIST OF PROPOSED BRIDESMAIDS.
WHAT DOES HE SAY?

A. "You have such great friends! Why wouldn't you? You're a wonderful person."
B. "Hot . . . Not hot . . . Hot . . . Hot . . . Not hot . . ."
C. "Do you think this one might be available for my bachelor party?"

YOU SAY THAT YOU'D REALLY LIKE TO LOSE 10 POUNDS BEFORE THE BIG DAY.
WHAT DOES HE SAY?

A. "Why? You look absolutely gorgeous!"
B. "Well, I don't think you need to, but if it makes you feel better about yourself,
let's go on a diet together."
C. Looking up from the *Sports Illustrated* Swimsuit Edition, he says, "You think ten is enough?"

YOU'RE DISCUSSING HOW TO TRAVEL BETWEEN THE CEREMONY AND THE RECEPTION. DOES HE SUGGEST . . .

A. A royal wedding carriage, drawn by trotting Clydesdales, driven by a top hat–wearing chauffeur?
B. His uncle's well-worn, but sentimentally important, '63 Cadillac convertible?
C. Hitching a ride in the back of the catering truck to save money?

WHAT IS HIS TOP PICK FOR A WEDDING GIFT REGISTRY?

A. Tiffany
B. Amazon
C. AutoZone

YOU'RE HAVING YOUR PRENUPTIAL MEETING WITH YOUR CHOSEN MARRIAGE COUNSELOR. HIS BEHAVIOR IS CHARACTERIZED BY . . .

A. Listening intently and offering good suggestions.
B. Saying, "Sure thing, pal!" and "I'm on it" a little too much.
C. Constantly checking ball scores on his iPhone.

WHO WAS THE FIRST PERSON HE CALLED AFTER YOU SAID YES?

A. His mom, and you heard him say, "Are you sitting down? I've got amazing news!"
B. The billing office at his gym, to cancel his membership, now that it's "in the bag"
C. Bachelor Parties R Us

WHO'S HIS FIRST CHOICE FOR BEST MAN?

A. Your brother
B. His brother
C. His frat brother, nicknamed "Toilet Breath"

WHEN HE SLIPPED THE ENGAGEMENT RING ON YOUR FINGER FOR THE VERY FIRST TIME, DID HE . . .

A. Stare longingly into your eyes—while his eyes welled up?
B. Perform a touchdown-style "victory" dance?
C. Mutter, "Well, maybe the third time's the charm"?

HOW DID HE PROPOSE TO YOU?

A. On a moonlit beach during a romantic Caribbean vacation
B. At your favorite neighborhood restaurant
C. By txt msg

WHAT MONTH DID HE SUGGEST GETTING MARRIED—AND WHY?

A. June, because it's traditional
B. September, for the beautiful fall weather
C. December, for tax purposes

WHAT WAS THE FIRST THING HE SAID WHEN HE MET YOUR MOM, AFTER YOU ANNOUNCED YOUR ENGAGEMENT?

A. "Now I have two moms! How cool is that!"
B. "I feel right at home with your family!"
C. "So, how long do I have before you turn into that?"

Porn Points

A = **3**

B = **1**

C = **-3**

19 to 36 POINTS
Consider yourself one lucky bride!

1 to 18 POINTS
Have him study *Porn for the Bride*.

-36 to 0 POINTS
SEE IF ANY OF HIS **GROOMSMEN** ARE SINGLE.

Finding out WHAT WOMEN REALLY WANT,
and getting that information into the public domain, has been the life's
work of the Cambridge Women's Pornography Cooperative.
Please help support our important scientific breakthroughs by sharing
these findings with friends, neighbors, and colleagues.

Go to our Web site, **WWW.WANNASNUGGLE.COM,**
to see and e-mail results from the original *Porn for Women* and
Porn for Women XXX (Hotter, Hunkier, and Handier around the House),
as well as our groundbreaking *Porn for New Moms* and
Porn for Women of a Certain Age. You can also buy our journals,
postcards, and pinup *Porn for Women* calendars!

Were you *inspired by these photos* to come up with a
PORN FOR WOMEN scenario of your own? Send it to us.
We may include it in a future study, and maybe it'll even get published
someday. That'll make you an honorary member of the
CAMBRIDGE WOMEN'S PORNOGRAPHY COOPERATIVE.

You bet

I DO!